The Learning Works

Create a Culture

A Complete Framework for Students to Use in Creating an Original Culture

Grades 5–8

**Written by Carol Nordgaarden • Illustrated by Bev Armstrong
Cover Art by Lucyna A. M. Green**

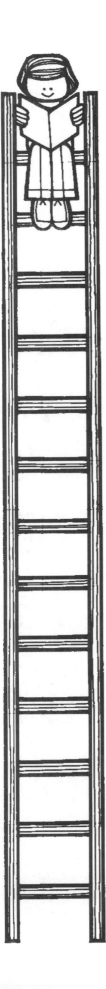

The Learning Works

Cover Art:
   Lucyna A. M. Green

Illustration:
   Bev Armstrong

Editing:
   Jan Stiles

Copyright © 1995
The Learning Works, Inc.
P.O. Box 6187
Santa Barbara, California 93160

ISBN: 0-88160-240-X

Contents

Project Ideas

Culminating Activities

Introduction

Create a Culture offers an exciting array of activities that will immerse students in all the elements that combine to make up a culture. The main objective is to increase students' understanding of what makes cultures unique, as well as to help them see and appreciate the similarities and differences that exist among cultures. By designing a fictitious culture and deciding its history, students will learn how cultures develop, change, and grow.

This unit is designed for cooperative learning groups of three to five students each. Work is done during class and as homework. The project can be completed in four to six weeks, depending on how time is used and how many activities are assigned.

Create a Culture is divided into four sections:

- Making Decisions
- Creating the Culture
- Project Ideas
- Culminating Activities

Making Decisions

These activities encourage brainstorming and note taking within each group. Students plan their fictitious cultures by using maps, geography texts, almanacs, encyclopedias, and atlases to answer questions in this section and to construct each culture's history and travels. Completing this section and the concluding group worksheets will enable students to move on to the next section of the project.

Creating the Culture

With these pages, the students of each group begin to construct how their new culture operates by reading about real cultures and applying the concepts to their fictitious one. As the teacher, you may decide to assign all of the activities included or to allow students to work on the sections they find most interesting and most applicable to their chosen time period or habitat.

> Some students may object to the "Religion and Rituals" activity. Although these concepts are basic to cultural identity, you may need to use your discretion and either group together those students who are sensitive to this issue or allow students to skip the activity if necessary.

The section ends with directions for reporting on the created culture by writing an "archaeological document."

Project Ideas

This section provides a chance for students to demonstrate their created cultures through multimedia and three-dimensional models, presentations, and other projects. You can manage these activities in three different ways:

- Have each group do all of the projects provided. This will require each student to take responsibility for several projects.

- Decide how many projects you want each student to complete and then select the specific projects you want each group to do. You could have every group do the same projects or give different projects to each group.
- Give all the project sheets to each group and let the students decide which ones they will do. You might also require all groups to do a particular project and then let each group choose its additional projects.

Whatever you decide, you should ensure that each student group uses a variety of project ideas so that the final cultural displays are more interesting. Students should be guided toward choosing the projects that showcase their talents as well as expand their skills.

Culminating Activities

This section includes directions for presenting each group's work to classmates, other students, family members, and people in the community. The teacher may use this section to help students plan an open house and/or displays for their own cultural museum. Formats for letters inviting guests to the open house are provided. You may also want to add a mini-lesson on writing letters and addressing envelopes.

Making Decisions

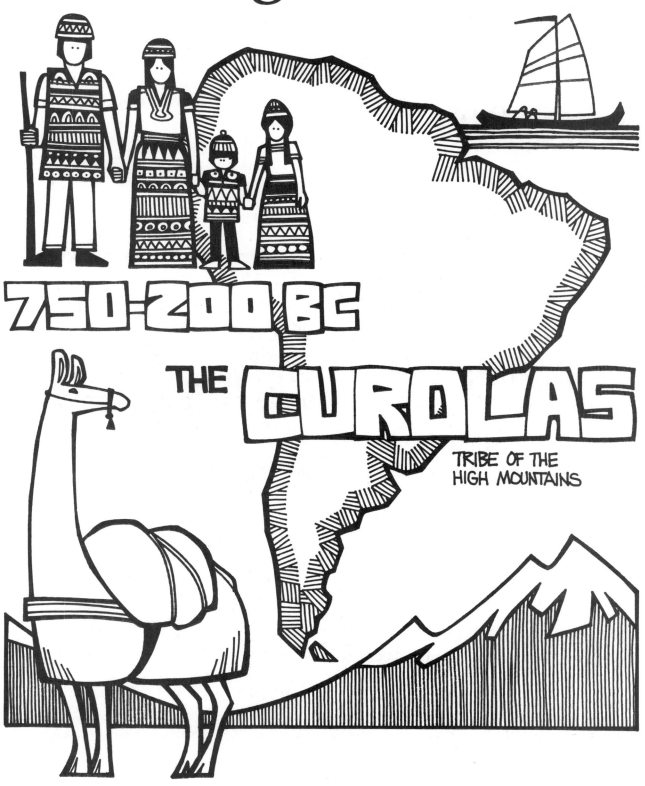

750-200 BC

THE CUROLAS

TRIBE OF THE HIGH MOUNTAINS

Name _____

Naming Your Culture

When people come together in one place, they must develop ways of behaving that allow them to live together as a group.

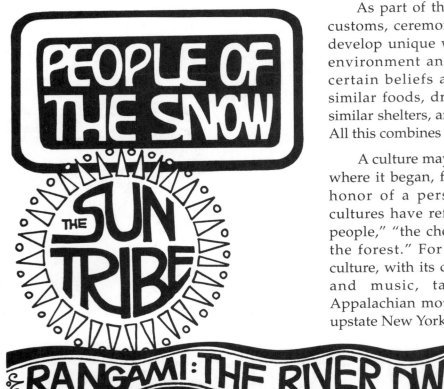

As part of that process, they devise laws, customs, ceremonies, and celebrations. They develop unique ways of understanding their environment and one another. They adopt certain beliefs and reject others. They eat similar foods, dress in the same style, build similar shelters, and share a common language. All this combines to form their culture.

A culture may take its name from the place where it began, from a particular belief, or in honor of a person or event. Members of cultures have referred to themselves as "the people," "the chosen ones," and "children of the forest." For example, the Appalachian culture, with its distinctive style of handicrafts and music, takes its name from the Appalachian mountain region that runs from upstate New York to Alabama.

List below some possible names for your culture. Explain briefly why each name seems appropriate.

1. _____
2. _____
3. _____
4. _____
5. _____

As a group, discuss each name listed. Then come to a consensus and select a name for your group's culture. Write your choice here.

_____

(You may decide to change this name in later activities. That's OK, but remember to write the new name here, too.)

Name _____

Historical Time Period

Environment, climate change, natural disasters, discoveries, new knowledge, encounters with other cultures, trade, war, ease of communication, and the migration or movement to a new location all become part of a culture's history.

The time period in which this history takes place determines how the culture develops. Much of U.S. culture is based on the ideals of seventeenth-century Europeans who first migrated to America in search of freedom and opportunity. In later years, however, immigrants who came from other nations brought new customs and ideas that also influenced U.S. culture.

Imagine that your culture had its origin in one area or region of the earth and then migrated to another. How did the time period of this migration affect the culture? Did maps exist? How rapid and sophisticated was communication with other cultures?

To understand the effects of time periods on cultures, find out about the periods below. Have each member of your group pick two or three periods to look up and describe to the rest of the group.

1. Ice Age
2. Industrial Revolution
3. Middle Ages
4. Neolithic Age
5. Twentieth Century

6. Renaissance
7. Bronze Age
8. Age of Discovery and Colonization
9. Victorian Age
10. Space Age

Name _____

Original Habitat

The place where a culture originates is its original habitat. Habitat refers to every aspect of the surroundings: the terrain or geography, the climate, the animals living in or passing through the area, and the plants growing there.

Every habitat has natural resources—from plants and rivers to minerals and building materials. Fertile soil for growing grain is also a natural resource. The people of a culture find ways to use the resources that occur naturally in their habitat. These resources may be necessary for survival, or they may offer a way for the culture to improve its way of life.

Trees, rocks, or mud may be used to build shelters. Grasses or leaves may serve as roofs to keep out the rain. Animals and plants may be used for food. Herbs may be gathered for medicines. Fur, skins, or feathers may be turned into clothing or ornamentation. Cultures also trade their natural resources for the resources of other cultures.

On this page, four very different habitats are pictured. Each offers different natural resources. The choice of resources will affect how people in each habitat live and shape their culture. Think about your culture's place of origin. Is it like any of these? What makes it unique?

Learn more about your culture's original habitat. On a world map, locate the place where your culture began. Use reference books to learn more about that location and the habitat it offered when your culture lived there. Remember that habitats can change, as in the cutting of the Amazon rain forest and the eruption of volcanoes on the island of Hawaii.

Name _____

Original Habitat (continued)

Answer these questions about your culture's habitat.

1. On what continent of the earth did your culture originate? _____

2. Where on that continent was your culture located? _____

3. What was the average summer temperature in that location at that time? _____

4. What was the average winter temperature? _____

5. What was the average annual rainfall in that location? _____

6. What was the landscape like? What were its common features? _____

   _____

   _____

7. What animal and plant life existed in this habitat? _____

   _____

   _____

Draw a map of the immediate area where your culture originated. Name and label the geographical features and the natural resources of the habitat.

Vocabulary: On the lines below, define the following terms.

1. culture _____

   _____

2. habitat _____

   _____

3. migrate _____

   _____

4. natural resource _____

   _____

Name _____

Reasons for Migration

Migration is the movement of people in a group or culture from one place to another. Migrations can be short or long—across a region, a continent, or an ocean.

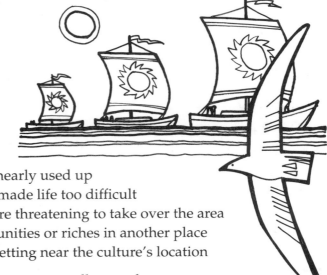

The factors that cause a culture to migrate play a part in determining the direction and distance of the migration and how the people of the culture view the experience. How long the migration took, the difficulties encountered, and the ingenuity and cooperation needed to make the trip all shape a culture's history and development.

The people of a culture might migrate because:

1. their natural resources are damaged or nearly used up
2. changes in the weather or climate have made life too difficult
3. neighboring cultures pose a danger or are threatening to take over the area
4. travelers have told tales of great opportunities or riches in another place
5. invaders sweeping across the land are getting near the culture's location

Sometimes individuals leave a culture and migrate as a small group because:

1. they no longer agree with the culture's leaders, rules, or customs
2. opportunities to succeed in their culture are denied them
3. they are sent or taken to a new location as prisoners, hostages, servants, or slaves

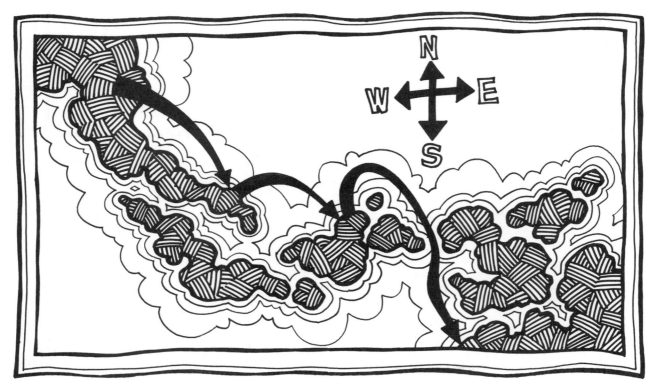

Name _____

Reasons for Migration (continued)

As a group, decide when and where your culture originated, when the group migrated, and where it settled after migrating. Write your decisions in the spaces below.

Time and place of origin:	Time of migration:	Final destination:

Use the lines below to explain why your culture left its original settlement.

_____

_____

_____

_____

_____

_____

_____

_____

_____

_____

_____

Create a Culture
© The Learning Works, Inc.

Name _____

Migration Route

The route a culture follows in its migration determines what kind of transportation the people will need and how long the migration will take.

If large bodies of water need to be crossed, the culture will need access to something that floats or flies. While many rivers can be forded on foot, others may present dangers such as hungry alligators, fast currents, or flash floods.

Mountains, too, present difficulties, and so do deserts. Harsh weather conditions can also threaten the culture's survival.

Areas controlled by other cultures can be dangerous to cross. In addition, if food and water are not available along the route, the people will need to find ways to carry these supplies with them.

Use maps to locate your culture's original habitat and its final destination. Decide the route the culture followed on its migration. Study your maps carefully. Then answer the following questions:

1. List any rivers or other bodies of water the people of your culture crossed in their migration.

   _____

2. List any mountains the people of your culture crossed over. _____

   _____

3. List any desert the people of your culture traveled across. _____

4. How long was this migration in miles? _____ in kilometers? _____

5. How long did this migration take? _____

6. At what time of year did the migration begin? _____ and end? _____

Name _____

Modes of Transportation

How a culture travels will depend on what it has available in its original habitat and what it has learned to use.

If a culture has no wheeled vehicles and never uses beasts of burden for riding or as pack animals, the people will travel on foot. This will take much longer than a modern-day move. A future migration to another planet, however, may take very long indeed.

For centuries, people have used animals for riding, carrying possessions, or pulling wagons, sleds, or litters. Horses, oxen, water buffalo, elephants, camels, llamas, reindeer, dogs, and others have been taught to work for people.

For land travel, cultures have built litters, sedan chairs, jinrikishas, covered wagons, coaches, trains, and cars. Crossing large bodies of water has called for other conveyances: canoes, rafts, junks, barges, kayaks, steamboats, sailboats, and planes.

As a group, decide the modes of transportation used by your culture. Check each one used and tell where and when the people used it. Make sure that the modes you choose actually were available when your culture originated and migrated.

❑ walking   Where did people usually walk and for what purpose? _____

_____

❑ beasts of burden   Which were ridden and/or used to carry goods or pull conveyances?

_____

❑ boats   How were they designed and made (of what materials)? _____

_____

❑ wheeled vehicles How were they designed and made (of what materials)? _____

_____

❑ other   How was the item made and used (describe the design, materials, etc.)?

_____

Name _____

Geography of the New Settlement

How do migrating people know when they have reached their final destination? In early times, they often didn't. They stopped because they liked what they saw, because a leader claimed to have had a "vision," or because the people were too tired or weak to continue.

Once a culture decides to stay, the people usually seek materials they can use to make shelters or buildings like those they left behind. They may build roads or canals, cut down forests, or clear rocks from the land.

Hunting cultures scout the paths of animals. Farming cultures begin clearing and planting fields. Farming cultures may even take familiar plants along on the migration. For example, early Polynesians emigrating by boat from Tahiti to the Hawaiian islands are believed to have brought their own food-bearing plants to grow in the new location.

Also, religious leaders may bring along the culture's shrines and artifacts to set up at the new location. Or they may create new shrines to honor the migration.

Cultures also take actions like raising flags or building monuments to honor the migration and arrival. With these actions, the culture claims the area and stamps its identity upon the new land. Some even drive out cultures already there or make them swear loyalty to the new culture.

Briefly describe one way that these cultures changed the geography of the places to which they migrated.

1. the ancient Romans who conquered much of Europe and England
2. homesteading families who migrated to the western territories of North America
3. American missionaries sent to Hawaii in the 1800s
4. miners and others who rushed west after the discovery of gold in 1849
5. the first generation of immigrants to Israel after World War II

Name _____

Geography of the New Settlement (continued)

As a group, discuss the geography of your culture. Consult reference books to find out the features of the terrain, the climate, the natural resources, etc. Record the information below.

1. On which continent did your culture settle after migrating? _____
2. Where on this continent do the people now live? _____
3. What is the average summer temperature? _____
4. What is the average winter temperature? _____
5. What is the annual rainfall? _____
6. What sources of water are available? _____
7. Describe all the geographical features and their locations (such as mountains, lakes, deserts, forests, etc.). _____

_____

_____

_____

_____

_____

_____

Name _____

Demographics of the People

Demography is the science of statistics and classifications for human populations. Demographic categories can include the size of a population, its rate of growth, and its density (the number of people in a given area). Other classifications include gender (male or female), age, status (married or single, employed or unemployed, etc.), education, life expectancy, income level, and more.

The different types of people within a population group all contribute to its identity. These groups may be national, regional, local, or cultural.

The people of a particular culture may exist in only one area, or they may live in many places throughout the world. For example, Hispanics, blacks, Jews, and others share common cultural backgrounds, yet they live in many cities in several different countries.

Today, many of the world's nations are made up of **subcultures**, or groups within a group. These smaller groups or subcultures may have a language, set of customs, or heritage that makes them distinct from the larger national group.

Research the countries listed below. Record the total population of the country and some of the different subcultures within each population.

	Population	Subcultures
1. Africa	_____	_____
		_____
2. Canada	_____	_____
		_____
3. China	_____	_____
		_____
4. Mexico	_____	_____
		_____
5. Spain	_____	_____
		_____
6. United States	_____	_____
		_____

Name _____

Demographics of the People (continued)

Within your group, discuss the demographics of the people in your culture after its migration.

Then, record your decisions about the demographic breakdown of your culture by filling in the blanks below.

Total population _____   Total male _____

Total female _____   Children under 3 _____

Males 3-10 _____   Males 11-20 _____

Males 21-65 _____   Males over 65 _____

Females 3-10 _____   Females 11-20 _____

Females 21-65 _____   Females over 65 _____

Within your group, decide what other demographic categories best describe your culture. Make a demographic chart to present the information you have selected. Categories you might include are family size, marital status, education, income levels, types of shelters, etc.

Create a Culture
© The Learning Works, Inc.

Name _____

Group Worksheet I

Have one person from your group fill in the final decisions your group made about your culture. Hand in this worksheet to your teacher when it is complete.

1. These are the students in our group (both first and last names): _____

_____

_____

_____

2. The name of the culture we created is _____

3. Historical time period _____

4. The migration of the people in our culture occurred during the year/years _____

5. Here is a detailed description of our culture's original habitat.

   natural resources: _____

   _____

   _____

   landscape features: _____

   _____

   _____

   _____

   climate: _____

   _____

   _____

Name _____

Group Worksheet II

Have one person from your group write three short paragraphs describing the final decisions
your group made about your culture's migration. Turn in the completed worksheet.

The name of our culture is _____

These are the reasons that the people in our culture migrated to their new habitat.

_____
_____
_____
_____
_____
_____

Our culture used these modes of transportation in the following ways during its migration.

_____
_____
_____
_____
_____
_____

Here is a description of the routes our culture followed from its original habitat to its new one.

_____
_____
_____
_____
_____
_____

Name _____

Group Worksheet III

Have one person from your group describe the final decisions your group made about the people in your culture and its location. Hand in this worksheet when it is complete.

Describe the geography of the new settlement, including the landscape, climate, and natural resources.

_____

_____

_____

_____

_____

_____

_____

Write a short paragraph detailing the demographics of the culture you are creating.

_____

_____

_____

_____

_____

_____

_____

_____

_____

_____

_____

_____

Creating Your Culture

Name _____

Living Quarters and Buildings

All people need some kind of shelter, whether they live in caves, tents, castles, or high-rise apartment buildings. The living quarters people choose show many things about their culture. The types of buildings people live in depend on the climate, natural resources, and social relationships.

In the 1500s, the Iroquois lived in **long houses** made from elm trees. A long house was 50 to 100 feet long and had a hall down the middle. A dozen or so families lived in separate parts of the same long house. People slept on wooden shelves along the walls and cooked their meals in the hall on open fires shared with other families.

In the Sahara Desert, people had to keep moving to gather food and to find fresh grass for their animals. These nomadic tribes lived in tents that they could carry with them and put up quickly at their next location.

Brainstorm with your group the answers to the following questions about shelter for the culture you are creating. Record your responses below.

1. What are the sizes, shapes, and styles of the houses where families live? _____

_____

_____

2. What are the rooms like where people gather? Where are these rooms located?

_____

_____

3. Where do people sleep? _____

_____

4. Where do people cook and eat their meals? _____

5. Are the houses communal or single-family dwellings? _____

Name _____

Living Quarters and Buildings (continued)

With your group, discuss the buildings your culture uses. Write a short paragraph answering each of the questions below.

1. What materials do people use to build their living quarters and other structures?

2. How are these buildings made, and who makes them?

3. To what building would people in this culture go for health care?

4. Where would people who had broken a law be sent?

5. Where would people go to be educated?

6. Where would they go to buy or trade goods?

7. Where would people gather for religious ceremonies?

Create a Culture
© The Learning Works, Inc.

Name _____

Family Structure

For some cultures, the entire tribe or group is much like a family, sharing work and food and helping to care for children. But even tightly knit cultural groups usually have smaller family units. There are three basic types of family structures.

1. **Patriarchal:** In this family or social structure, the father, or patriarch, is the head of the family. He makes the rules and decisions. In the absence of a father, the patriarch might be a grandfather or a respected uncle. In a patriarchal society, men are the leaders, and the descent is traced through the father's line. This is why women, upon getting married, have traditionally taken their husband's last name.

2. **Matriarchal:** In this family or social structure, women, or matriarchs, have the greater authority. Throughout history, there have been a number of cultures in which women have played a more powerful role than men. Among the Iroquois and Navajo, for instance, many women hold positions of leadership and set rules that govern family and community. In matriarchal family structures, descent is traced through the mother's family line.

3. **Egalitarian:** This term refers to families where the mother and father make decisions jointly and equally.

These terms also describe families.

1. The **nuclear family** refers to the parent or parents and children living together.
2. The **extended family** includes relatives like grandparents, aunts, and uncles who are close to the family but don't live in the same home. Most nuclear families also have an extended family.
3. In some cultures, the **tribal group** is also a kind of extended family.

Name _____

Family Structure (continued)

In your group, brainstorm answers to the following questions to describe the family structure in the culture you are creating.

1. What is the family structure in your culture? _____

2. What is the typical family size, and who belongs to this group? _____
_____

3. What roles do elderly people play in the family life of your culture? _____
_____

4. Check any activities that would be done by one specific family member in your culture. Tell who would be responsible for each task you checked.

❑ building _____

❑ cooking _____

❑ child care _____

❑ defense _____

❑ clothes making _____

❑ discipline _____

❑ education _____

❑ food gathering or hunting _____

❑ cleaning _____

❑ storytelling _____

Name _____

Power Structure

Nearly all cultures develop structures that give some people power over others. In families, for instance, parents have the power to discipline and teach their children. Government is another power structure. Throughout history, many forms of government have been tried.

Aristocracy is government by a small, privileged class, usually wealthy or educated or respected members of the culture.

Democracy is a government in which people vote for leaders to represent them and to pass laws and decide policies.

Monarchy is rule by a king or queen who gains power by being born into a royal family or by marrying royalty.

Oligarchy is rule by a small group of people who select themselves as leaders.

Plutocracy is a government controlled by a culture's wealthiest members.

Theocracy is a government controlled by a culture's religious leader or leaders.

Dictatorship is a type of government in which one individual holds power and makes all political and military decisions. Dictators often seize power with the help of armed followers.

Totalitarianism is the belief that every aspect of government, work, education, the arts, science—in fact, all of life and thought—must match the beliefs of those in power.

Look up the countries listed below. Find out what form of government each one has, or had.

Iran (before 1900) _____   Venezuela (1850-1935) _____

Iran (after 1979) _____   Greece (8th century B.C.) _____

Japan _____   Nepal (before 1980) _____

Vatican City _____   Russia under Stalin _____

Tudor England _____   United States _____

Name _____

Power Structure (continued)

Brainstorm with your group to decide who holds power in your culture. Record your decisions by answering the following questions.

1. What form of government does your culture have? _____

2. How are leaders selected? _____
   _____

3. What are the titles of those in power? _____
   _____

4. What are the responsibilities of those in power? _____
   _____

5. What ceremonies are held when a new leader is named? _____
   _____
   _____

6. Is there a written record of laws in your culture? _____
   • What is it called? _____
   • Does your culture have a constitution to describe how the government functions? _____
   • Does the constitution apply to everyone, including those in power? _____

7. How are arguments or legal disputes settled? _____
   _____

8. What major laws have been made and why? _____
   _____
   _____

9. What punishments exist for rule breakers? _____
   _____

Name _____

Economy and Currency

Nowadays, most of us take for granted that whatever we need is a quick shopping trip away. We go to a variety of stores and simply hand over money that we or other members of our family have earned in exchange for all kinds of goods and services.

It sounds so simple, and yet it's anything but. Our way of life is based on a complicated economy. An economy refers to the way people use resources to make and sell goods and services. Before economies developed, money didn't exist. People had to produce everything for themselves. Because this was too difficult and time consuming, a barter system began. In other words, people traded goods or services they had for ones they didn't have but needed.

The introduction of money as medium of exchange allowed economies to grow. Today each country has a currency and a "national economy." The United States, for example, has a "free enterprise" economy. Privately-owned businesses produce and distribute most of the goods our society needs on a daily basis. The people in a free enterprise economy earn money by owning or working for the businesses that produce and deliver goods and services.

Not every country has a free enterprise economy. In socialist or communist economies, for example, the government – not private businesses – controls the production and distribution of goods. In these economies, most people work for and get paid by the government.

Write the name of the country that uses each of the coins listed below.

franc _____   guilder _____

drachma _____   krone _____

quetzal _____   rial _____

rupee _____   yuan _____

Name _____

Economy and Currency (continued)

Brainstorm with your group how the economy of your new culture works. Discuss your ideas and answer these questions. Record your decisions below.

1. What items are considered valuable and why? _____
   _____
   _____

2. Who has access to these things of value? _____
   _____
   _____

3. What types of "cash" are used? _____
   _____
   _____

4. How does trade within this culture happen? _____
   _____
   _____

5. How do people display their wealth? _____
   _____
   _____

6. Who is considered "successful"? Why? _____
   _____
   _____

On a separate sheet of paper, design a currency for your culture.

Name _____

Education

Cultures must develop ways to pass on important skills, traditions, and knowledge. Parents often teach their children these things, but children also learn from a variety of other teachers.

Since the people of many early cultures could neither read nor write, oral storytelling was a common way to preserve the culture's history and pass it on to the next generation. For example, a Mandinkan *griot* or storyteller taught the tribe's history to its children.

Today, most cultures rely on books, as do schools in the United States and Japan. In Japan, however, the school day is much longer. Many young Japanese also go to classes outside of school. Pressure to pass difficult tests that decide the kind of high school or college students are allowed to attend keep these classes in demand.

The city-state of Sparta in ancient Greece had a very different idea of education. Because victory in war was valued above everything, boys had to leave home at age seven and join groups run by army officers. Until the age of 18, boys walked barefoot, slept on hard beds, and worked at gymnastics, running, jumping, javelin and discus throwing, swimming, and hunting. Meals were small to encourage boys to steal food. Failures were harshly punished, and boys were taught to take pride in the pain they could endure. Girls lived at home but also learned to throw a javelin and discus, run, jump, and wrestle.

With your group, discuss education in your culture. List some of the things children would need to learn at each of the ages below.

1. Ages 2 to 5 _____
2. Ages 6 to 10 _____
3. Ages 11 to 13 _____
4. Ages 14 to 18 _____
5. Over 18 _____

καλοδιδάσκαλος

Name _____

Education (continued)

Brainstorm with your group how the culture you are creating educates its people. Have one person in your group fill in the following information.

1. How do the people in your culture learn about its history? _____

    _____

    _____

2. At what age do children begin their education? Are children educated individually or in a group? _____

    _____

3. How many hours do children spend in a formal learning situation each day? During what hours? _____

    _____

4. Who are the teachers in this culture, and what methods do they use to teach? _____

    _____

    _____

5. How do children learn to survive in the environment? What survival skills must they learn?

    _____

    _____

6. What social skills are valued by this culture? How are these skills taught? _____

    _____

    _____

    _____

7. What are some of the unique things about education in your culture? _____

    _____

    _____

    _____

    _____

Create a Culture
© The Learning Works, Inc.

Name _____

Language

People communicate in many ways. Members of a culture will use their own language to communicate within the group, but they may also know several other languages.

For example, a person living in Scotland may speak Gaelic. A person living in Canada may speak French or English or both. People in Switzerland might speak Italian, German, and French.

People who live in different regions of the same country may speak the same language but pronounce the words differently. They are said to have accents, like the Boston or Southern accent, or an Irish **brogue**.

When members of a group have their own special words or phrases or use standard words in odd ways, their speech is called **dialect**. Cockney in England is one example. Nonstandard vocabulary or informal usage that is popular for a limited time is called **slang**.

Sometimes language is not even meant to be spoken.

List below some ways that people communicate.

1. _____

2. _____

3. _____

4. _____

5. _____

Name _____

Language (continued)

Brainstorm with your group all the different ways people in your culture communicate. Then fill in the following information.

1. What is the name of the language your culture speaks? _____

2. About how many words exist in your culture's vocabulary? _____

3. List the major ways in which your culture communicates. _____
   _____
   _____

4. What are some examples of slang or dialect within your culture? _____
   _____
   _____

5. Write six important words from your culture's vocabulary, just as they would appear in a
   dictionary. Include the pronunciation, part of speech, and definition for each.

   (a) _____
   _____

   (b) _____
   _____

   (c) _____
   _____

   (d) _____
   _____

   (e) _____
   _____

   (f) _____
   _____

Create a Culture
© The Learning Works, Inc.

Name _____

Religion and Rituals

For many cultures, religious beliefs help shape the society's customs and laws. This is especially true in cultures where the people hold the same religious beliefs or where the leader of the culture is also the leader of the religion.

Religious rituals and celebrations usually become important parts of a culture's identity, even when the people in the culture have different beliefs. Often, the laws and system of government will reflect how the culture views and deals with religion.

Research these religions and find out what cultures believe in them. Then record one thing about each religion that makes it unique.

1. Buddhism: believers _____

   unique quality _____

2. Christianity: believers _____

   unique quality _____

3. Hinduism: believers _____

   unique quality _____

4. Islam: believers _____

   unique quality _____

5. Pantheism: believers _____

   unique quality _____

6. Quakerism: believers _____

   unique quality _____

7. Shinto: believers _____

   unique quality _____

8. Judaism: believers _____

   unique quality _____

Name _____

Religion and Rituals (continued)

Brainstorm with your group and record your answers to the following questions about your culture's religion and rituals.

1. What god(s) is/are worshipped by the people in this culture? _____
   _____

2. What are the most important teachings, principles, or ideas that the god(s) represents?
   _____
   _____

3. How do the people show respect for their god(s)? _____
   _____

4. Who are the "holy people" in this culture? _____
   _____

5. What are the duties of these "holy people"? _____
   _____

6. What are the privileges of these "holy people"? _____
   _____

7. What role do animals play, if any, in religious rituals? _____
   _____

8. Describe the most important religious holiday in your culture. Tell why it is important and
   what people do to celebrate it. _____
   _____
   _____
   _____
   _____
   _____

Name _____

Heroes and Heroines

All cultures have heroes and heroines, people who are respected for having done remarkable things. Often, these heroes become part of the stories told in the culture.

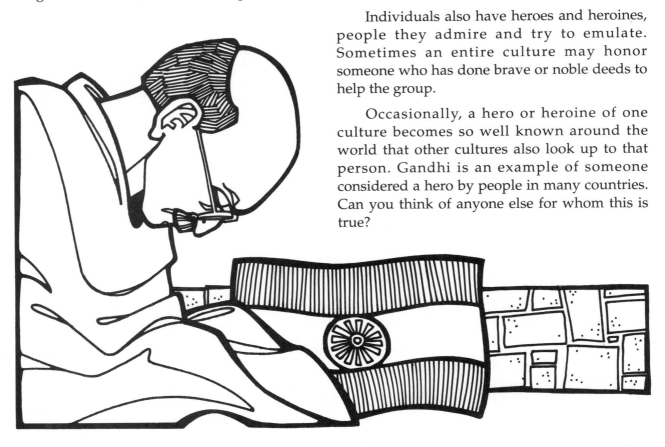

Individuals also have heroes and heroines, people they admire and try to emulate. Sometimes an entire culture may honor someone who has done brave or noble deeds to help the group.

Occasionally, a hero or heroine of one culture becomes so well known around the world that other cultures also look up to that person. Gandhi is an example of someone considered a hero by people in many countries. Can you think of anyone else for whom this is true?

In the boxes below, name a person in each profession who could be considered a hero or heroine in today's society.

scientist	philanthropist	athlete

educator	physician	other

Name _____

Heroes and Heroines (continued)

Brainstorm with your group the heroes and heroines in the culture you are creating. Then answer these questions.

1. What are the names of the heroes and heroines in your culture? _____

   _____

   _____

2. Write a short description of the remarkable things each one did that made the person heroic.

   _____

   _____

   _____

   _____

   _____

   _____

   _____

   _____

   _____

   _____

3. How does your culture honor its heroes and heroines? _____

   _____

   _____

4. What values or important ideas does each hero or heroine represent in your culture? Write the people's names and what value or idea each person represents.

   a) _____

   b) _____

   c) _____

   d) _____

   e) _____

Name _____

Folklore

Remember the tale of George Washington chopping down a cherry tree? That story is one example of **folklore**, a body of stories reflecting a culture's beliefs, traditions, heroes, and values.

Often, the characters of folk tales represent admired qualities that are passed on in stories told to children. Some folk tales are made-up stories about real people, like George Washington and Johnny Appleseed (John Chapman). Others are told about bigger-than-life, make-believe heroes, like Paul Bunyan and Pecos Bill.

Folk tales have been told for centuries. All cultures have them. The Baganda tribe of East Africa, for example, has a collection of stories so old that no one knows when they originated. One character, the clever and resourceful Wakaima rabbit, closely resembles Brer Rabbit, hero of the tales told by black Americans in the 1800s. Coyote, the trickster of Native American tales, is another example of a folk tale character who exemplifies cleverness and cunning.

At one time, all folklore was part of an **oral tradition** passed on by word of mouth. Today, folklore finds its way into poetry, song lyrics, and fables. How did you learn the story of George Washington and the cherry tree? What cultural quality does his action symbolize?

Have each person in your group read a different Aesop's fable and then do the following:

1. Tell your group which fable you read and what its moral was.
2. Retell your fable to the others in your group.

As a group, do the following:

1. List the similarities that exist among all the fables you heard or read. _____

_____

_____

2. List the differences. _____

_____

_____

Name _____

Folklore (continued)

With your group, brainstorm ideas about the folklore of your culture. Fill in the information below.

1. List three behaviors, qualities, or traits that the people in your culture consider important.

   a) _____

   b) _____

   c) _____

2. In some folk tales, the same character is repeated, like Robin Hood and Merlin of English stories, the centaurs of Greek legend, and the tales of the Norse hero Peer Gynt. List below the character or characters who would appear in many of the folk tales told in your culture.

   _____

   _____

   _____

   _____

Create a Culture
© The Learning Works, Inc.

Name _____

Holidays and Celebrations

A holiday is a day made special by a culture's customs or laws. Usually, some kind of celebration is held on that day.

Holidays help a culture remember and honor its history. Each culture develops its own traditions for recognizing and celebrating these special days. People have parades, sing special songs, go on picnics, give gifts, eat special foods, or have pageants.

Do research to learn more about each of these holidays celebrated around the world. Name the culture where the holiday originated and describe one unusual fact about the day.

1. Kwanzaa _____

_____

2. Bastille Day _____

_____

3. Angin Matsui _____

_____

4. Diwali _____

_____

5. Dia del Idiome _____

_____

6. New Fire Holiday _____

_____

7. Shavuot _____

_____

Name _____

Holidays and Celebrations (continued)

Brainstorm with your group some of the holidays your culture celebrates. For ideas, review previous sections about the people, beliefs, or events that are important in your culture. Record your decisions about four of your holidays below.

What is the holiday called?	**How is it celebrated?**	**Why is it important?**
1. _____	_____	_____
2. _____	_____	_____
3. _____	_____	_____
4. _____	_____	_____

Name _____

Dance

Dance is an important part of most cultures. Some dances are created to celebrate historic events. In the hula, a Polynesian dance, the dancers use pantomime to retell these events.

French Gavotte

Sometimes dances stand for something else, like hunting, prayers, or warfare. In these symbolic dances, people may take on the traits of an animal. Other dances are purely for entertainment, like square dancing and couples dancing.

Often, special clothing is worn for the dance. Hula dancers wear flower leis and long skirts of grass. In Scotland, both men and women dancers wear **kilts**, pleated wool skirts with plaid designs that represent a clan or family.

Latin Flamenco

Israel's Hora

Use references to look up each of the dances pictured above. Write a few sentences about each dance, explaining why it is performed and what special clothing is worn.

1. Flamenco: _____

_____

_____

2. Gavotte: _____

_____

_____

3. Hora: _____

_____

_____

Name _____

Dance (continued)

Brainstorm with your group some of the ways your culture uses dance to celebrate its history or identity. Plan at least two of the dances, using the lines below.

First Dance	**Second Dance**

name of dance _____   name of dance _____

special clothing worn _____   special clothing worn _____

_____   _____

_____   _____

_____   _____

_____   _____

event celebrated _____   event celebrated _____

_____   _____

some of the steps or movements in the dance   some of the steps or movements in the dance

_____   _____

_____   _____

_____   _____

_____   _____

_____   _____

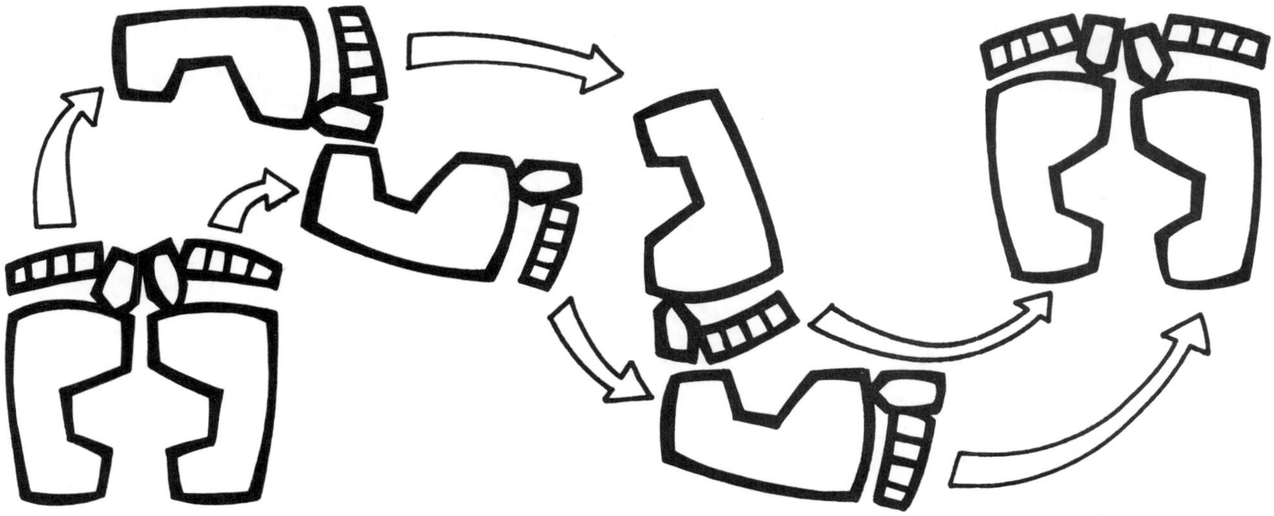

Create a Culture
© The Learning Works, Inc.

Name _____

Foods and Their Preparation

Each culture develops a diet and ways of preparing food based on what is available in the culture's habitat. Many cultures can be recognized by the unique foods they eat or by their characteristic ways of cooking or seasoning meals.

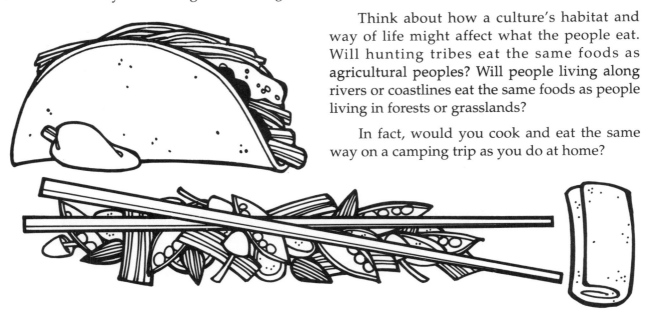

Think about how a culture's habitat and way of life might affect what the people eat. Will hunting tribes eat the same foods as agricultural peoples? Will people living along rivers or coastlines eat the same foods as people living in forests or grasslands?

In fact, would you cook and eat the same way on a camping trip as you do at home?

Research the following foods. Tell where each originated and list the main ingredient needed to make each one.

1. borscht _____

2. chimichanga _____

3. escargot _____

4. goulash _____

5. couscous _____

Name _____

Foods and Their Preparation (continued)

Think about your created culture's natural resources. Decide what would be eaten by the people and how food might be prepared. Brainstorm with your group, and then answer the following questions.

1. What are three special foods that the people in your culture eat regularly? _____
    _____

2. Who is in charge of getting the ingredients, and how do they get them? _____
    _____

3. What tools or weapons are used in this process? _____
    _____

4. How many meals a day are eaten and at what times? _____
    _____

5. Who prepares each meal, and where is this done? _____
    _____

6. Who gathers to eat these meals? _____
    _____

7. Are there any special activities, manners, or rituals that are part of the meals? If so, describe
    them. _____
    _____
    _____

8. Are any foods used as treats or rewards? If so, describe them. _____
    _____
    _____

9. Do any people in your culture sell food to make money? If so, who are these people, and what
    do they sell? _____
    _____
    _____

10. Does your culture engage in trade with other cultures for food that is not found locally? _____

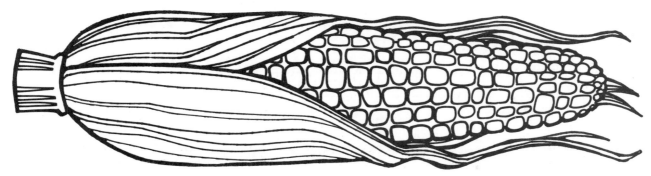

Name _____

Clothing

Most cultures have special clothing that is different from what they wear every day. For instance, to show respect for the dead, people who are mourning in Ghana wear **kobene**, cotton dyed a deep red. In many western cultures, men wear tuxedos and women wear long and sometimes elaborate dresses for formal occasions.

Clothing is also determined by climate and natural resources. Some northwestern Native American tribes made ornamental capes and hats from cedar bark. Cultures in arctic climates wore parkas, mittens, and boots made of sealskin and lined with fur.

Throughout history, people also have worn uniforms that tell what kind of work they do, like today's chefs, soldiers, nurses, or firefighters.

In the space below, describe the clothes people in your culture wear for each special event listed. Include the colors and the materials, and tell which people wear this special clothing.

1. weddings _____

   _____

   _____

2. funerals _____

   _____

   _____

3. first holiday (name) _____

   _____

   _____

4. second holiday (name) _____

   _____

   _____

5. a special occupation _____

   _____

   _____

Name _____

Rites of Passage

Rites of passage are ceremonies held to honor important milestones reached by members within the cultural group.

When these accomplishments or new stages of life are recognized, the family—or even the entire culture—may join in a traditional celebration to honor the event. People may wear clothing associated with the rite of passage, prepare special foods or drinks, and perform traditional dances or ceremonies.

The ceremonies can recognize a variety of events: reaching a certain age, getting engaged or married, having a child, completing an education, winning a competition, etc. Some rites of passage mark major changes in a person's life. Others are less significant but still play significant roles in the life of the culture.

Brainstorm with your group to decide what rites of passage exist in your culture. Describe below the rites you have chosen.

birth _____

coming of age _____

marriage _____

death _____

others (name each one) _____

_____

_____

_____

_____

Pick one of the rites of passage listed above and find out how three real cultures celebrate this milestone. Pick from an African, European, Asian, or Hispanic culture. Tell the others in your group what you have learned.

Name _____

Calendar

Every culture has some way of marking the passage of time. Ancient cultures used the sun and moon to count the passing of days and months. Today, we use calendars, clocks, and watches.

Think about how the people of a culture might measure time. Would they count rotations of the earth or phases of the moon? Hours on a clock or shadows on a sundial? Years or the changes of seasons?

What names might people give to parts of the day, month, or year? What about longer time periods? Would people refer to a decade, the person in power, a war, an event, a major invention, or a natural disaster like a flood or an earthquake?

How might a culture's habitat, way of life, religious beliefs, heroes and heroines, or traditions affect the way people think about time? What role might scientists or astronomers play in learning about time?

With your group, discuss the different ways your culture keeps track of time. Decide the names of different time segments. Consider the climate, geography, people, and beliefs of your culture. What effects might they have on your calendar?

Make notes with your group. Then use the next page to create a calendar for your culture.

Name _____

Calendar (continued)

Create a calendar for your culture. Divide the space below into the blocks of time your culture uses on its calendars. (Rotate the page or use the page more than once if you prefer.) Label holidays and special events. Show how your calendar can be used for record keeping and planning.

Name _____

Toys, Games and Sports

People in a culture often participate in sports and play games to fill their leisure time.

In the United States, baseball is known as "the great American pastime." Soccer is considered the national sport of many South American and European countries. Games like chess are popular worldwide.

Often games—or sports—grow out of tournaments that highlight strengths or skills needed in the culture. Members of tribes, rival towns, or countries compete to prove their superiority. The ancient Greek Olympics, Medieval jousts, and early American lumberjack contests are a few examples.

With your group, decide some of the toys people play with in your culture. Record your decisions below.

1. What kinds of toys are popular? _____
_____

2. What materials are used to make most toys, and who makes them? _____
_____

3. Do any of these have a purpose other than for entertainment? _____
_____

4. Describe three toys that are popular in your culture and tell who plays with each one.

    a) _____

    b) _____

    c) _____

Name _____

Toys, Games and Sports (continued)

Brainstorm with your group the games people in your culture play in their leisure time. Record your answers to the following questions.

1. What games do family members play together? _____
   _____

2. What games are played by a solitary player, not a group? _____
   _____

With your group, decide what kind of team competition sports are played in your culture. Answer the questions below.

1. Do any of these games have a purpose other than entertainment? Describe any special purpose.
   _____
   _____

2. What are the main rules for one of the games? _____
   _____
   _____
   _____

3. How many are on a team for most games? _____

4. What are the players' roles? _____
   _____
   _____

5. Who is eligible to play? _____
   _____

6. Do the players wear special clothing or uniforms? If so, describe them. _____
   _____
   _____

7. Where is each kind of game played? _____
   _____

8. Who is invited to watch the games? _____
   _____

9. How are winners determined? _____
   _____

10. How are winners rewarded for winning? _____
    _____

Name _____

Defense and Protection

Most cultures have some system of defense. They want to protect territory and valuables from neighboring cultures. Wars have been fought because one culture trespassed on another's land.

Some cultures try to prevent this kind of invasion. People have built walls, forts, and castles. They have dug moats and ditches, invented weapons, and trained armies.

Sometimes the landscape itself can be part of a culture's defenses. Castles may be built on high cliffs, or cultures may migrate to islands that are not easily reached by others.

Describe briefly at least three ways that people around the world defend themselves and their property.

_____

_____

_____

_____

_____

_____

_____

_____

Name _____

Defense and Protection (continued)

Brainstorm with your group the answers to the following questions. Record your ideas below.

1. Which features of the landscape make your culture easy to attack? _____
   _____
   _____

2. What defenses does the landscape provide naturally? _____
   _____
   _____

3. Which people in your culture are trained to defend it? _____
   _____

4. How are defense strategies taught, and who teaches them? _____
   _____
   _____

5. Have any major battles been fought? If so, who was involved and who won? _____
   _____
   _____
   _____

6. What types of weapons are used in training and fighting? _____
   _____
   _____

7. What other ways do the people in your culture defend themselves? _____
   _____
   _____

8. What kinds of clothing or uniforms do the defenders wear? _____
   _____
   _____

Name _____

Reporting About Your Culture

An **archaeologist** is someone who studies past cultures by analyzing the remains of their buildings, bones, and **artifacts**, such as tools, dishes, and other items used by the people in the culture.

Now that you have recorded the elements of your culture, you will publish a more detailed archaeological report. Each person in your group will write one or more sections for this report.

Once all the sections have been written, edited, and revised, you will put them together in one comprehensive report. Then write a cover letter for your report using the model on page 58.

Follow these steps:

1. In your group, decide who will write about each of the topics listed below.
2. Write that person's name next to the topic, along with the date the work is due.

	Name	**Date Due**
• living quarters and buildings		
• family structure		
• power structure		
• economy and currency		
• education		
• language		
• religion and rituals		
• heroes and heroines		
• folklore		
• holidays and celebrations		
• dance		
• food		
• clothing		
• rites of passage		
• calendar		
• toys, games and sports		
• defense and protection		

Name _____

Reporting About Your Culture (continued)

Each person in your group should do the following for each of his or her topics:

1. Write one to two pages about each of the topics assigned.
2. For each topic, write a detailed description of that aspect of his or her culture.
3. Edit, proofread, and revise.

You can put the sections of your archaeological report together in any order you choose. With your group, decide the order you will use. List that order below.

1. _____
2. _____
3. _____
4. _____
5. _____
6. _____
7. _____
8. _____
9. _____
10. _____
11. _____
12. _____
13. _____
14. _____
15. _____
16. _____
17. _____

Create a Culture
© The Learning Works, Inc.

Name _____

Cover Letter Worksheet

Use the letter format below when you write the cover letter for your report.

_____
(school name)

_____
(street address)

_____
(city, state, zip)

_____
(date)

Science Times Magazine
10000 Culture Avenue
Discovery, CA 00001

Science Times:

    The _____ culture, which existed from _____ to _____ , has recently been discovered.

    A group of eminent archaeologists, namely _____
_____
_____

has examined the artifacts of this newly discovered culture and has arrived at some extremely important conclusions.

    The attached scientific document is the result of very thorough and painstaking research. Included are discussions of the following topics about this culture:

_____
_____
_____
_____
_____

    Won't you join us in celebrating this historic discovery?

Sincerely,

_____

Project Ideas

Name _____

Making Maps and Logging the Journey

You have been chosen as a travel reporter for your culture. Show the migration of the people of your culture by making a map that traces the journey from the culture's original habitat to its final destination.

Next, draw a map of the group's new settlement.

Also, create a journal that describes reactions to key events that occurred during the migration. Make your travel log or journal look and sound authentic.

For your maps, you could . . .
- put details or pictures on your maps to illustrate the original habitat and the new settlement
- make a three-dimensional settlement map or model
- age the paper with lemon juice

For your journal or log, you could . . .
- fill in the brainstorming chain below to plan your culture's adventures before you begin writing
- age your paper by wrinkling it, fraying the edges, leaving it in the sun, or using lemon juice
- draw pictures to illustrate events
- make a container to hold the log
- use fabrics to write on or to cover the log

MIGRATION OF THE CATODONS

Left original habitat	Migration event	Migration event	Migration event

Migration event	Migration event	Migration event	Arrived at final destination

Name _____

Designing Clothing

Yοu are your culture's head clothing designer. Review the natural resources in your new settlement and any work your group did on the culture's ceremonial dress. What materials are available to you as the culture's clothing designer?

Illustrate five to seven different outfits worn by your people. Include both ceremonial and everyday wear.

For your clothing presentation, you could . . .

- sew examples for classmates to model
- dress dolls in the clothing
- draw designer sketches and label each one
- make large paper dolls with a variety of outfits

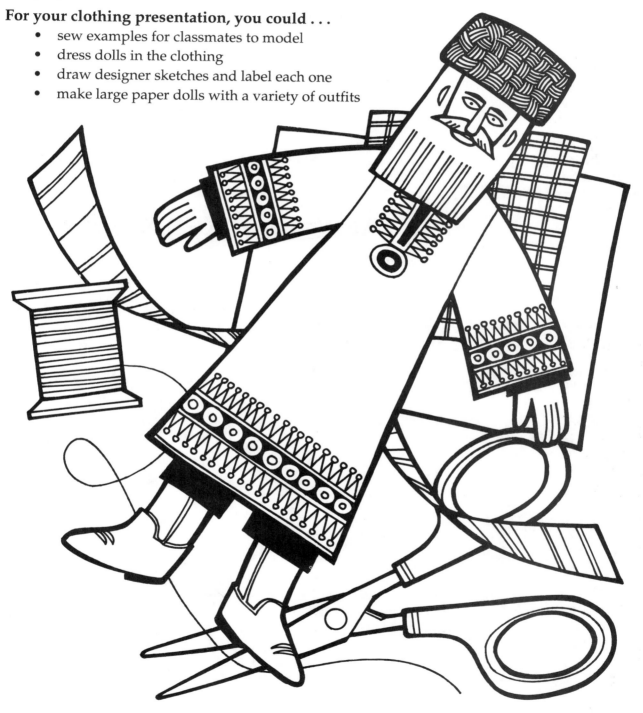

Name _____

Crafting Jewelry

You are your culture's jeweler. Review the natural resources in your habitat to see what is available for your craft.

Design and make three to five pieces of jewelry. Be sure to design items for people to wear with both ceremonial and everyday clothes.

For your jewelry presentation, you could . . .

- illustrate and label each accessory
- write display cards explaining the special meaning of each piece, if any
- recreate the ceremonies when jewelry is worn
- work with the clothing designer to coordinate styles and colors
- make and label a display of the stones and materials your culture uses in its jewelry

Name _____

Writing an Anthem

You are the songwriter for your culture, and the people want an anthem.

Write the words to an anthem for your culture. Make sure the anthem refers to the history and qualities of your people. Your new anthem should be at least 25 lines long.

For the presentation of your anthem, you could . . .

- mount the lyrics on an illustrated poster
- tape-record someone performing the anthem
- teach your class to sing or chant the anthem
- write music to go with the words and then teach your group to sing your anthem

Heroes confirmed in our conquests, Lands that with riches abound, Freedom both now and forever: Let all the earth hear this sound!

Name _____

Creating Totems

Some cultures create statues or totem poles that represent beliefs, stories, or important figures from their pasts. Animals, plants, objects found in nature, and even people can be included in a totem.

You are the totem maker for your culture. Design a totem pole that includes three to five different symbols from your culture's history. Your totem pole should be detailed, colorful, and large enough to be seen easily from across a room.

For the presentation of your totem pole, you could . . .

- determine how big to make the totem pole by deciding where it will be located in the settlement
- make an even larger version of the totem pole
- work with the jeweler to include totem designs in the culture's jewelry
- have the jeweler design ceremonial jewelry to put on the totem pole
- act out some of the events or ceremonies represented on the totem pole

Name _____

Designing Flags and Pennants

You are the flag maker for your people. Design and make a flag or pennant to represent your culture. This flag should be large enough to be seen from several places within the settlement.

You may also want to design one or two smaller flags or pennants that identify special groups in your culture, like a sports team, the army, the leader of your culture, etc.

For the presentation of your flag and/or pennants, you could . . .
- consult your group to decide on symbolic colors for your culture and then use them in making your flag
- display your flag while singing your culture's anthem
- hold a parade or a flag-raising ceremony
- make smaller versions of the flag to hang around the room, or use your special pennants that identify sports teams, the army, etc.

Name _____

Telling Fables

You are your culture's official storyteller. Review the characters, morals, and values your group decided on when creating your culture's folklore.

Write and illustrate two or more fables based on the beliefs, heroes, and history of your culture. Each fable should be two to three pages long.

For your fables, you could . . .

- illustrate each page (see *Aesop's Fables* for examples)
- bind your fables together into book form
- act out one or more fables as plays
- pretend to be a storyteller sharing one of your fables with a group of children
- videotape a reenactment of one or more of your fables

Name _____

Crafting Toys and Games

You are your culture's toy maker. Review the notes your group took about your culture's sports and leisure activities. Use those ideas to make some toys and games.

There are two parts to your job: (1) create and teach two games played in your culture, and (2) make at least one toy used by children in their leisure time. Be sure to illustrate the games and write out their rules so you can teach others how to play.

For your presentation of toys and games, you could . . .
- create and wear team or game uniforms, if appropriate
- display the rules and moves for each game on a poster
- write the history of the game
- have classmates play with the toy(s) you have created
- build a model of the structure or court where the game is played

Name _____

Writing Your Bill of Rights

The Constitution of the United States contains a Bill of Rights that guarantees American citizens certain freedoms and protections. Read a copy of the Bill of Rights and think about how the document reflects the values of America.

You are your culture's government recorder. Review the notes your group took on the type of government your culture has. Then, write the Bill of Rights for your people. The document should include at least ten rights or freedoms the government guarantees the people. Make your Bill of Rights as authentic in appearance as you can.

For your Bill of Rights, you could . . .

- age the paper with lemon juice
- exhibit the "original document" in a special container
- have your group memorize and recite your Bill of Rights
- act out a signing ceremony

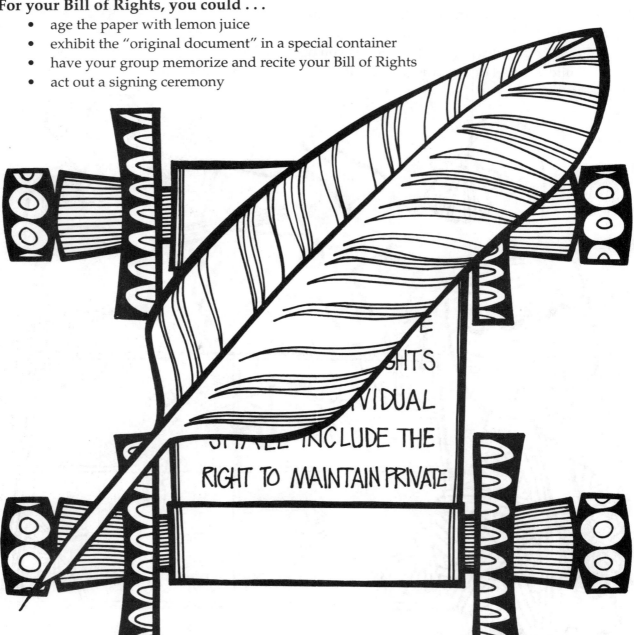

Name _____

Making Music and Musical Instruments

You are your culture's musical composer. Design and make a musical instrument and write a few paragraphs explaining how your instrument is made, who uses it, and when it is used.

Then compose a song you can play on your instrument. You can compose your song with or without lyrics, but make it unique to your culture.

For your musical presentation, you could . . .
- work with the person writing the anthem so you can set it to music
- use your song as background music during the reenactment of an event, ceremony, or the migration
- write a song that is played or sung on one of your culture's special holidays
- teach a classmate to play a song on your musical instrument

Create a Culture
© The Learning Works, Inc.

Name _____

Choreographing Dances

You are your culture's **choreographer**, or dance creator. Review the material your group put together about dancing in your culture.

Make up the steps and movements to at least two of the dances performed by the people in your culture. Be ready to teach these dances to your classmates.

For your dance presentation, you could . . .

- name each dance
- explain the purpose of each dance
- make posters showing the steps of each dance
- teach the dances to your class
- videotape the dances and play the videotape for your class
- hold a dance contest

Name _____

Arranging Hairstyles

In many cultures, hair is worn in certain ways for a ritual or as part of a costume for a performance. Some cultures have unique everyday hairstyles as well.

You are your culture's hair stylist. Design at least six hairstyles worn in your culture for ceremonies and/or for everyday. Include styles for males and females of all ages. You should also design hair accessories, if appropriate.

For your presentation of hairstyles, you could . . .
- model each style using a wig or a doll
- use your classmates as models
- sketch each style and explain when it is worn and by whom
- bring enough materials for your classmates to make hairstyle accessories using the ones you designed as models

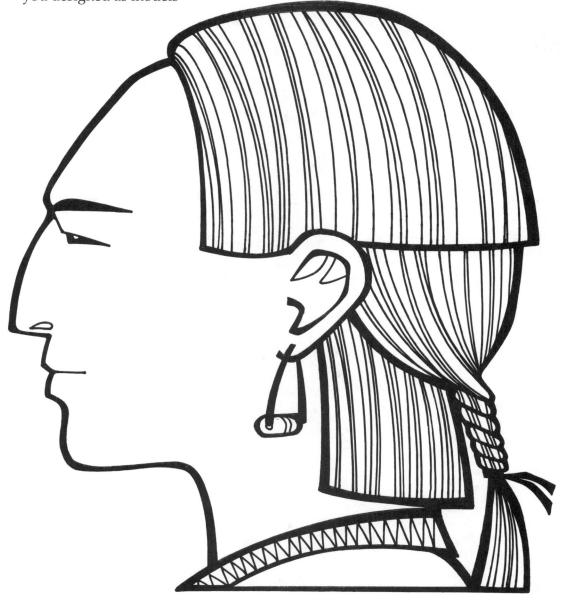

Name _____

Profiling People

Yₒu are your culture's biographer. Your role is to write about at least two people who are or were important in your culture.

Tell, in story form, about the life or contributions of each person. Use the person's name as the title of each profile. Each of your profiles should be at least one page long.

For your presentation of famous people, you could . . .

- bind your character profiles in book form
- illustrate each profile with pictures and drawings
- draw a family tree for each person and create posters for display
- take the role of a person profiled and make a videotape of a speech or event from the person's life

Name _____

Penning Poetry

You are your culture's official poet. Write three poems about any people, places, or events important to your culture.

One kind of poem you might write is a **cinquain,** an unrhymed poem that has five lines and a specific structure. A cinquain pattern and example are shown below.

noun (topic)	Borulu
adjective, adjective, adjective,	learned, wise, respected,
-ing word, -ing word, -ing word,	teaching, searching, sharing,
descriptive phrase about the topic	storyteller to all small children
noun (a synonym for topic)	Wisdom

For your poems, you can use the cinquain structure above or any poetic form that is familiar to you. You also may want to research different forms of poetry and then write an epic poem, a sonnet, free verse, or haiku.

For your poetry presentation, you could . . .

- put your poems on poster board for display
- bind your poetry into book form
- illustrate each poem with pictures or cultural designs
- memorize and recite each poem
- choose one of your poems and explain its significance or tell why it's popular or important in your culture

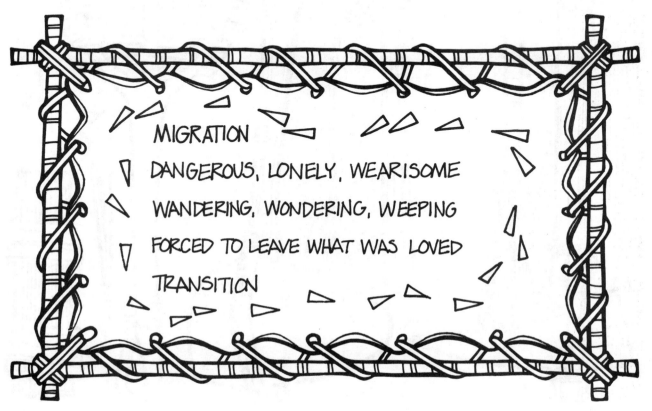

MIGRATION
DANGEROUS, LONELY, WEARISOME
WANDERING, WONDERING, WEEPING
FORCED TO LEAVE WHAT WAS LOVED
TRANSITION

Name _____

Inventing Tools

You are the culture's toolmaker. Review the material about life in your culture and about its geography to determine the resources available to you. Then design and make at least five tools used by your people.

Include in your "toolbox" items used for preparing food, building houses, making clothes, making toys, making the culture's currency, writing and recording information, and gathering or growing food.

For your presentation of tools, you could . . .

- label and describe each tool
- tell what each tool is for and who uses it
- demonstrate each of your tools to show how it is used
- build a toolbox for your tools
- have classmates use the tools to do or make something

Name _____

Designing Architecture

Yᴏu are your culture's official architect. Review your group's work concerning the types of buildings and building materials used by your culture.

Build models of a family dwelling and at least one other important building in the settlement. Be as detailed as possible, and make sure each building is labeled for display.

For your architectural presentation, you could . . .

- make blueprints of the floor plans
- mount your models on sturdy wood for transport
- use dolls or miniatures in the models to show how people use the buildings
- show the environment surrounding each building
- show several buildings in a diorama

Name _____

Developing Transportation

You are your culture's transportation officer. Look back over the work your group did to decide the modes of transportation people in your culture used when they migrated.

Build or draw and label at least five vehicles, roads, bridges, watercraft, or other transportation modes and routes unique to your culture.

For your transportation presentation, you could . . .
- demonstrate each vehicle
- sail model watercraft in a container of water
- use dolls or toy animals in your demonstration
- build a life-sized model of a vehicle and teach classmates how to use it

Name _____

Promoting Communication

You are your culture's chief of communications. Review the work your group did on education, language, folklore, and anything having to do with communication.

Demonstrate how the people in your culture communicate by doing these three activities: (1) record and define at least six key words from your culture's vocabulary, (2) create and display two important cultural symbols, and (3) demonstrate at least one form of communication, other than talking face-to-face, that is used by your people.

For your presentation on communication, you could . . .
- make a dictionary that contains your words and their definitions
- make a poster showing body movements that are meaningful in your culture and explaining what they mean
- teach your words and/or movements to the class
- write and perform a **pantomime**, or play without words, that uses symbols and movements

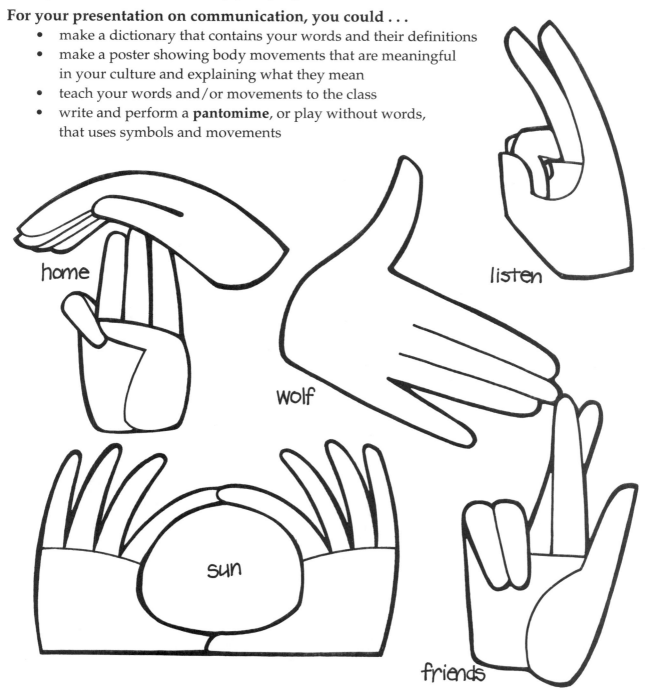

home

listen

wolf

sun

friends

Name _____

Planning Your Oral Presentations

Each group will take a turn presenting its culture to the class. Plan to use your artifacts and archaeological report to tell about your culture.

Your group will also use this time to demonstrate its games and dances and to present any reenactments, videotapes, etc. Use this page to plan the presentation you will make to the class.

Find out from your teacher the length of time you have to present your culture to the class. Use the space below to note the date and time of your group's oral presentation and to plan the sequence in which you will share your information. Estimate and record how much time each topic will take.

Date of presentation: _____ Time: _____ to _____

sequence of topics	**estimated time**
1. _____	_____
2. _____	_____
3. _____	_____
4. _____	_____
5. _____	_____
6. _____	_____
7. _____	_____
8. _____	_____
9. _____	_____
10. _____	_____
11. _____	_____
12. _____	_____
13. _____	_____
14. _____	_____
15. _____	_____
16. _____	_____
17. _____	_____
18. _____	_____
19. _____	_____
20. _____	_____

Culminating Activities

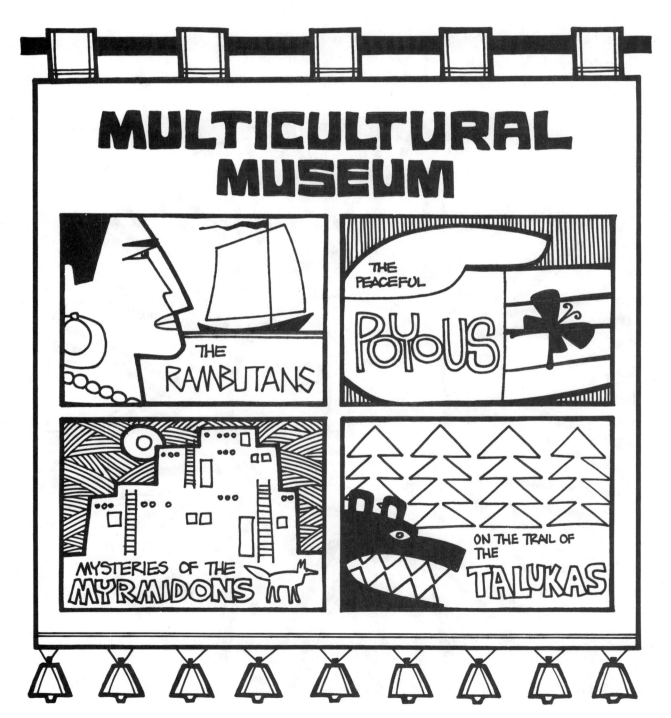

Name _____

Evaluation Form for Oral Presentations

After each group's oral presentation, answer the following question. On a separate piece of paper write your answers in complete sentences.

1. What is the name of the culture you just learned about?
2. What more would you like to learn about this culture?
3. What was the most interesting part of this group's presentation?
4. Were the presenters well prepared and organized?
5. Describe one thing that each presenter did exceptionally well.
6. Write one or two recommendations that you think would improve this group's presentation for the open house.

Name _____

Planning the Cultural Museum

As a class, design a cultural museum to display the artifacts and archaeological reports for the cultures you have created.

With your teacher, discuss the rooms you could use on your campus (library, auditorium, multipurpose room, etc.) and select the best available location for your museum. Once your choice is confirmed, write it here.

The room we will use is _____

Next, you need to decide where in the museum each culture will be displayed. If you plan to set aside a separate area for reenactments and demonstrations, agree on where it will be.

In the space below, make a diagram of the room you will use. Label the area where each culture will be displayed, and mark off a separate demonstration space, if you plan to have one.

Museum Floor Plan

Name _____

Your Museum Display Plan

Now that you know where the museum will be located and what section of the room will be set aside for your culture, plan with your group how you will use the space assigned to you.

Discuss the following questions and write your answers below.

1. Where will your artifacts be placed? _____

_____

_____

2. How will each artifact be displayed, and who will make signs or explanatory materials?

_____

_____

_____

3. What demonstrations or reenactments will be performed, and who will perform them?

_____

_____

_____

4. Will these performances be live or shown on videotape? _____

5. What media assistance will you need, if any? _____

_____

Who will provide the assistance? _____

What arrangements do you need to make? _____

_____

On a separate sheet of paper, sketch or write the plans for your display in the cultural museum. Include where and how your archaeological report will be displayed.

Name _____

Open House Plan

When your cultural museum is ready to be viewed, you'll want to invite others to see it.

As a class, discuss who from your school you want to invite to the open house for your museum.

List people or classes from your school here:

1. _____
2. _____
3. _____
4. _____
5. _____

Discuss who you would like to invite from your family.

List the names of family members here:

1. _____
2. _____
3. _____
4. _____

Decide who you would like to invite from your community.

List the names of people from the community here:

1. _____
2. _____
3. _____
4. _____

With your teacher, plan when you will hold your open house. Once you have decided the date and time, fill in the information below.

Date of open house _____

Time for open house: from _____ to _____

Place _____

Address _____

_____

_____

Name _____

Open House Invitation

Here is a sample letter you can copy to invite people to the open house for your cultural museum.

Using the guest list on page 83, divide up the letters you need to write to people from your school and community. Each of you will write the letters to invite your own family members. Keep track of who will be attending.

Name of school
School's address,
followed by the date

Guest's name and address
(three lines)

Dear _____ ,

    The _____-grade class of _____ School created our own cultures.
        (grade)   (name of school)

To do this we learned about other cultures and about the components that make up a culture

(geography, government, etc.). We will be holding an open house in which we will display our

work in a cultural museum. We would like you to attend. The open house will be held from

_____ to _____ in the _____ of our
    (time)   (time)   (room)

school. We hope you can be there.

Sincerely,

_____
(your signature with your printed name below it)

(You can also print your title for your culture below your name: for example, Architect of the

_____ Culture, Poet of the _____ Culture, etc.)

Name _____

Venn Diagram: Comparing Cultures

Compare your created culture to your real culture by completing the Venn Diagram below.

List in the right-hand circle all the things that make the culture you created different from your real culture.

List on the left all the things that make your real culture different from the one you created.

In the center segment, list all the things both cultures have in common.

Thinking Skill: Comparing and Contrasting

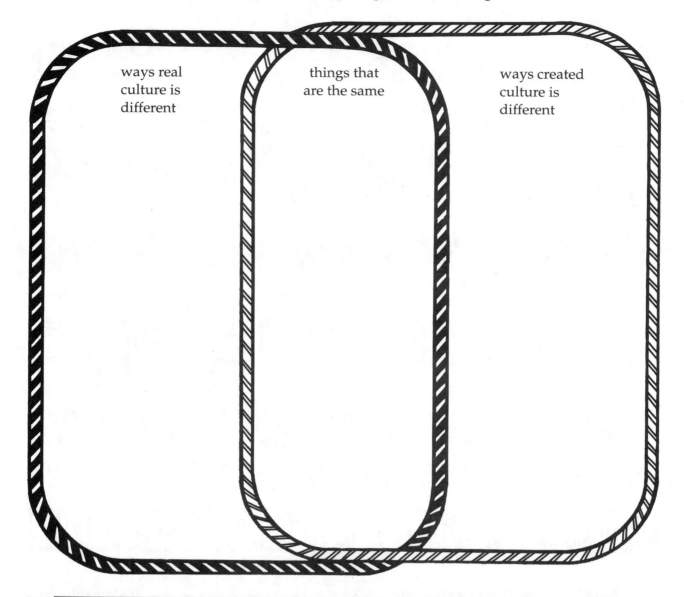

ways real culture is different

things that are the same

ways created culture is different

Congratulations on completing *Create a Culture!*

Create a Culture
© The Learning Works, Inc.

Cultural Clip Art

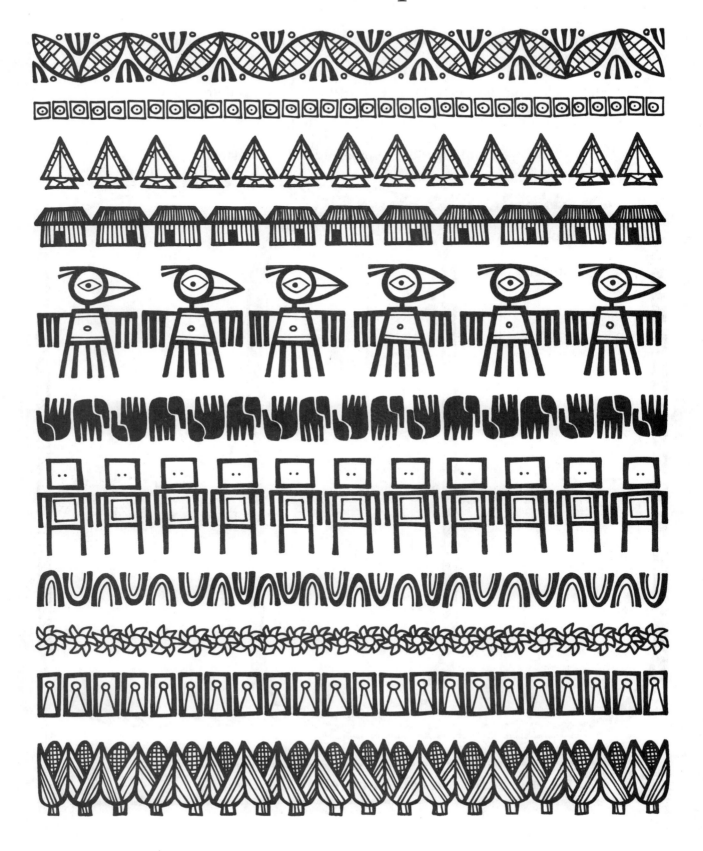

Cultural Clip Art

Cultural Clip Art

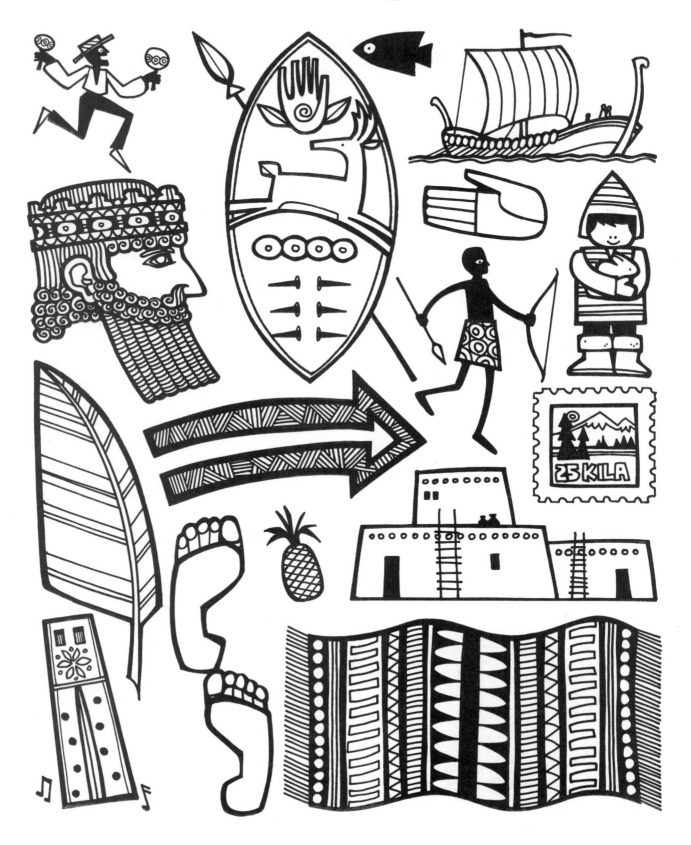